THE LITTLE BOOK OF
WEED

FSC
www.fsc.org

MIX
Paper | Supporting
responsible forestry
FSC® C020056

Published by OH!
20 Mortimer Street
London W1T 3JW

ISBN 978-1-91161-052-6

Editorial: Chris Caufield
Project manager: Russell Porter
Design: Tony Seddon
Production: Rachel Burgess

A CIP catalogue record for this book is available from the British Library

Printed in China

10 9 8 7 6 5 4 3 2

THE LITTLE BOOK OF

WEED

A GUIDE FOR THE
CURIOUS & THE CONNOISSEUR

CONTENTS

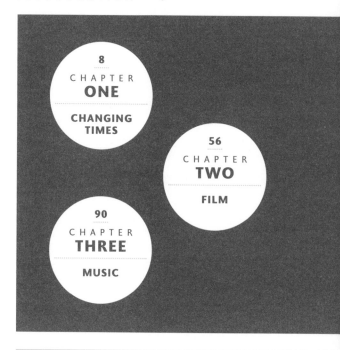

INTRODUCTION

Marijuana or cannabis use (or any and all other names it is known by) is an emotional subject for many people. Some argue that cannabis is a relatively non-toxic herb that can be used as medicinal treatment, whilst others believe it represents the first step towards addiction and despair by introducing people, particularly young people, to the world of Illicit drugs use. Whatever name it's known by, it incites debate on every level.

This Little Book gives you practical and historical information on its various uses cases throughout its history, and includes quotes and commentary made by a variety of personalities, historians, authorities, and analysts on this interesting and prolific herb.

Ganja, weed, cannabis, Mary Jane, blunt, chronic. The nicknames for marijuana are as numerous and varied as the users it appeals to. Grown in fields and hotboxes around the world, weed's influence on culture extends far beyond teenagers trying pot for the very first time or chronic hippies fully immersed in the lifestyle.

Howlers from politicians struggling to balance reality with perception, hilarious stand-up comedians in smoke-filled clubs, musicians whose albums defined eras, and movies that put it all on film owe much of their infamy to the herb.

Weed's impact on culture is explored throughout this Little Book as musicians from Bob Marley to the Beatles share their insights. Then there are the movie masterpieces, and missteps, that put marijuana front and centre, as well as the comedians who based their acts on its illicit properties.

Weed's ever-changing legal status, and how we got here, is also examined, making this book ideal not just for budding musicians or movie buffs, but for all those with an interest in how cannabis achieved its mythic status in certain (smoke) circles.

Bill Hicks asks: "Why is marijuana against the law? It grows naturally upon our planet. Doesn't the idea of making nature against the law seem to you a bit… unnatural?"

The Little Book of Weed looks at marijuana use, from its first-ever references to parents naming their children after their favourite varietals, and asks the same question.

So sit back, chill out and roll up roll up for *The Little Book of Weed* as it emblazons the leaf's legacy across its 192 pages.

CHAPTER
ONE

CHANGING TIMES

Humans have been using cannabis for more than 4,000 years.

The cannabis plant originated in central Asia before being introduced to other parts of the world.

Easy to cultivate, it was used to make clothing, paper and rope, and as a herbal medicine to treat conditions such as malaria, constipation and rheumatism.

The main psychoactive "ingredient" in weed is Tetrahydrocannabinol – more commonly referred to as THC. In short it's the THC that gets you high.

There is some evidence
that ancient cultures understood
the mind-altering effects
of cannabis.

The residue of burned
cannabis seeds have been
discovered in tombs in China
dating back to 500 BC,
showing that people inhaled
combusted cannabis plants.

In ancient India, cannabis is mentioned in the sacred Hindu texts known as The Vedas, compiled between 1500 and 1000 BC.

According to these writings, cannabis was one of the five sacred plants. Its leaves are described as a source of happiness, and a means of helping us to shrug off fear and anxiety.

In the fifth century, the historian
Herodotus described in his
Histories how a nomadic tribe
called the Scythians used cannabis
smoke to purify themselves after
burying their dead.

In the West, the use of cannabis as a medicine began to grow in the mid-19th century. By 1900, it was available as an "over counter" medicine for ailments such as a cough.

Queen Victoria was said to have been prescribed cannabis by her doctor to help her with period pains.

Towards the end of the 19th
century, the syringe was invented.

Injected drugs take effect
more quickly but since cannabis
can't be dissolved in water, it
can't be injected.

The discovery of drugs such
as aspirin further added to the
decline of cannabis for
medical use.

In 1928, marijuana was made illegal in the UK. It followed an international drugs conference in Geneva where the Egyptian delegate convinced the room that cannabis was as dangerous as opium.

However, doctors were able to prescribe cannabis for medical use until 1971 when the Misuse of Drugs Act was passed.

In Prohibition America, cannabis was legal, while alcohol was illegal.

The head of the Bureau of Prohibition, Harry Anslinger, was appointed as the head of the Federal Bureau of Narcotics, and once alcohol was taken off the blacklist he went after weed.

In 1930, Anslinger sought the views of 30 leading scientists; 29 said cannabis did no harm, one said it did. That was the view Anslinger put to the press.

Source: Lee Dalloway, "Nine things you probably didn't know about marijuana", BBC, 20 April 2017

In 1937, President Franklin D. Roosevelt signed the Marihuana Tax Act (yes, that's how marijuana was spelt back then).

It marked a turning point in the country's attitude to cannabis and formed the basis of future laws.

In the UK, weed, really took
off in the 1950s when Caribbean
immigrants began to arrive in
the country.

On the night of 15 April 1952,
London's Metropolitan Police
carried out the UK's first drugbust
at the Club Eleven nightclub
in Soho, leading to the arrest of
several young British men. This
put an end to assumptions that
drug use was confined to the
lower classes and non-whites.

In the 1960s, the flower power movement that had its roots in America and later spread to western Europe promoted the use of drugs like cannabis as a way of expanding consciousness.

"

There is no evidence that this activity is causing violent crime or aggression, anti-social behaviour, or is producing in otherwise normal people conditions of dependence or psychosis requiring medical treatment.

"

Wootton Report, a Home Office investigation into the effects of cannabis, 1968

The first-ever internet
transaction over the world wide
web was to buy marijuana
in the 1970s.

Source: John Markoff, *What the Dormouse Said:
How the Sixties Counterculture Shaped the
Personal Computer Industry*, 2005

In the UK, cannabis was reclassified as a type C drug in 2004, lowering the criminality associated with it. This followed a study by the Advisory Council on the Misuse of Drugs.

In 2009, it was elevated back to Class B, meaning the maximum penalties increased to five years for possession and 14 years for supply. However, the Advisory Council on the Misuse of Drugs stands by its study.

In November 2018, UK law was changed to allow doctors to prescribe medicinal cannabis products under certain circumstances.

Cannabis oil can be used to treat conditions such as severe epilepsy and cancer.

And now for the science part...

THC is the chemical secreted by the glands of the marijuana plant, particularly around its reproductive organs, as well as the bud glands or flower.

In marijuana, the THC chemical is used to ward off parasitic predators, bacteria and viruses. In humans, it gets you stoned.

When smoked, the THC in the plant gets released into the blood stream and reaches the brain within seconds.

It then mimics naturally occurring cannabinoid chemicals and attaches itself to your cannabinoid receptors.

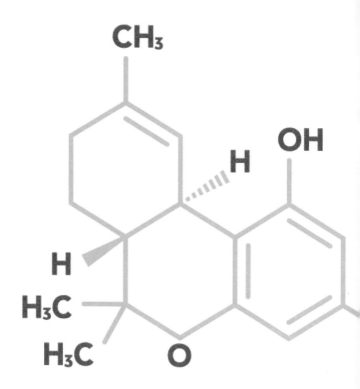

The molecular structure
of THC – particularly
decarbonized THC – fits
perfectly with the brain's
neurotransmitters, which
the body uses to carry
information around.

CH₃

All weed is different. Yup,
each crop is as unique as the
fingerprints you are leaving all
over this book.

This is because the growing
conditions, environment and
genetic make-up of the strand of
cannabis all contribute to how it
ends up.

Much like wine.

Exactly how high you get depends on the length and strength of your hit, and how you administered it.

Any weed that has a THC level higher than 20% is regarded as being very strong and will knock your socks off.

On the other hand, eating raw cannabis will do precisely nothing to get you high. That perfectly formed molecular structure has to be created – with heat.

But highs aside, it has been argued that raw cannabis has plenty of health benefits, so you may still want to eat it!

Heating cannabis "decarboxylates" it, removing carbons to create its new potent form.

Preparing Weed

Decarbed cannabis works well in cookery – as long as you're cooking for yourself!

But, before you can create any dish, you have to prepare your weed, to make an oil or butter.

Here's
how...
· · · · · · · · · · · · · · · ·

1 Preheat your oven to 110C/230F.

2 Break up your dried bud into small pieces.

3 Spread the pieces on a baking sheet.

4 Bake the bud for 35 minutes, moving the cannabis around every 10 minutes to ensure even toasting.

5 After 35 minutes, check the cannabis. It should be a light-brown colour. If it's not, put it back in for another five minutes. Keep an eagle eye out so you don't burn your bud.

6 Remove the baking sheet and set it aside to cool.

7 Put the baked bud in a food processor and pulse until the weed is coarsely ground.

Making Cannabutter

1 Boil about 1 litre/2 pints of water.

2 Add 450g/1lb butter and allow to dissolve.

3 Add 30g/1oz of your decarbed cannabis and lower the temperature to a very gentle simmer for two to three hours.

4 Strain through a cheesecloth.

5 Store in a refrigerator for six hours. This will allow the butter to rise and separate from the water.

6 Remove the butter.

Cannabutter can be stored in a freezer for about a month.

Perfect
Hash
Brownies

Ingredients

185g/6½ oz cannabutter

185g/6½ oz dark chocolate

100g/3½ oz milk chocolate,
chopped

85g/3oz plain flour

40g/1½ oz cocoa powder

3 eggs

275g/10oz caster sugar

1 teaspoon vanilla extract

1. Slowly melt the cannabutter over a low heat and stir in the dark chocolate until it's combined into a smooth paste before removing from heat and allowing to cool.

2. Sieve flour with cocoa powder into a bowl.

3. In another large bowl, mix eggs, sugar and vanilla extract. Then add your cannabutter and chocolate mix.

4 Fold in the flour and cocoa powder mix, and add the chopped milk chocolate.

5 Line a baking tin and pour in the mixture.

6 Bake at 180C (350F) for 35–40 minutes until a shiny crust has formed. Allow to cool.

Enjoy with one of the movies listed in Chapter 2.

66

The illegality of cannabis is outrageous, an impediment to full utilization of a drug which helps produce the serenity and insight, sensitivity and fellowship so desperately needed in this increasingly mad and dangerous world.

99

Carl Sagan, "Mr X", *Marihuana Reconsidered*, 1971

"

Why is marijuana against the law? It grows naturally upon our planet. Doesn't the idea of making nature against the law seem to you a bit... unnatural?

"

Bill Hicks

❝

We all need something to help us unwind at the end of the day. You might have a glass of wine, or a joint, or a big delicious blob of heroin to silence your silly brainbox of its witterings but there has to be some form of punctuation, or life just seems utterly relentless.

❞

Russell Brand, *My Booky Wook*, 2007

"

I have always loved marijuana.
It has been a source of joy and
comfort to me for many years.
And I still think of it as a basic
staple of life, along with beer and
ice and grapefruits — and millions
of Americans agree with me.

"

Hunter S. Thompson

66

Sniggerette, *Noun*
A tab containing a quantity of
happy baccy. A spliff.

99

Viz, Roger Mellie, *Roger's Profanisaurus*, 2003

66

Weed-loving parents name daughters Sativa and Indica after marijuana strains.

Headline on metro.co.uk, by Jessica Lindsay, 12 February 2020

99

66

Pro-drug reform campaign group Transform says the government is denying that cannabis has medical uses while at the same time overseeing 'the world's biggest government-licensed medical cannabis production and export market'.

99

"Is the UK the world's biggest exporter of legal cannabis?", BBC Online, 2018

66

Ninety five tonnes of marijuana
was produced in the UK in 2016
for medicinal and scientific use,
accounting for 44.9 per cent of
the world total.

99

United Nations International Narcotics
Control Board, 2018

CHAPTER
TWO

FILM

Cannabis was made illegal around the world at much the same time that cinema was taking off as a medium. As such, it is not very surprising, when looking through a list of the greatest ganga films ever made, to see very few crop up in the format's early years.

In the 1930s, films tended
to be government-tilted
propaganda stories about the
horrors of drugs and the
"no-gooder" they would turn
you into.

It is not really until we get to the counter-culture movement of the 1960s that marijuana began to become more regularly featured in film.

Whether it was life imitating art or the other way around is the age-old debate.

As the era of flower power came to an end, cannabis was again vilified, and portrayed as a corrupt influence on society.

Even in the 1980s, any references to cannabis tended to come from historical pieces set around the "summer of love".

All that changed in the 1990s,
however, as lawmakers
began to re-examine the
herb's properties and question
legislation.

Now, hardly a day goes
by without a movie making a
reference to the drug.

"

A new and deadly menace lurking
behind closed doors. Marijuana,
the burning weed with its roots
in hell. In this film you will see
the ease with which this vicious
plant can be grown in your
neighbour's yard, rolled into
harmless-looking cigarettes.

"

Trailer, *Reefer Madness*, 1936

66

Captain America: Do this instead.

George Hanson: Oh, no thanks.
   I got some store-bought right
   over here on my own.

Captain America: No, man. This
   is grass!

George Hanson: You mean
   marijuana?

Captain America: Yeah.

George Hanson: Lord have mercy,
   is that what that is?

99

Easy Rider, 1969

"

The first commercially animated feature film to capitalize on the X rating it snagged from the Motion Picture Association of America to sell tickets. No joke, *Fritz the Cat* was made for $850,000 and bagged $90 million.

"

Den of Geek, 2018, describing the 1972 animated film
Fritz the Cat (a cartoon about a feline who,
after smoking some strong marijuana in Harlem,
hallucinates – and it all goes downhill from there).

66

Pedro: Man, what is in this shit, man?

Man Stoner: Mostly Maui Waui man, but it's got some Labrador in it.

Pedro: What's Labrador?

Man Stoner: It's dog shit.

Pedro: What?

Man Stoner: Yeah, my dog ate my stash, man.

99

Up in Smoke, 1978

"
That was my shoe, I'm so wasted.
"

On being asked over the phone how much
he's smoked, Sean Penn's character, Jeff Spicoli,
responds by slapping a shoe on his head.
Fast Times at Ridgemont High, 1982

"

Both of them are sad clones of a movie character: Jeff Spicoli, sketched so spookily by Sean Penn in *Fast Times at Ridgemont High*. Bill and Ted differ from Spicoli, their 'stoner' predecessor, only in that there are no drug references here to account for their allegedly jocular lack of ambition or interest in education or self-improvement.

"

Chris Willman on *Bill and Ted's Excellent Adventure*, *LA Times*, 1989

"Man"

Said a total of 203 times in the film
Dazed and Confused, 1993, where the
characters spend a considerable amount
of time getting high

"

It's one of the Number One
movies you check out when
you're baked.

"

Ice Cube looks back on *Friday*, his 1995 stoner hit
comedy, *Rolling Stone*, 2015

" I continue Hunter's work by bringing awareness of marijuana laws that target minorities and destroy families all over this country for possession of this plant. The 'Red Shark' is a symbol of our journey. **"**

Anita Thompson, Hunter S. Thompson's widow, in an interview with *ForbesLife* after donating his car to Cannabition – a 835-square-metre (9,000-square-foot) museum dedicated to cannabis, August 2018

**
Saving Grace begins with a familiar sound: a deep breath, sharp intake, pause, then a slow, satisfied release.
**

Julie Buckles on *Saving Grace* in *Cannabis Culture*, 2000

66

After 25 years of being fake
weed dealers, it feels nice to be
real weed dealers.

99

Kevin Smith on the launch of three new varieties
of weed ahead of the long-awaited launch of
the *Jay and Silent Bob* sequel, *The Hollywood Reporter*,
28 September 2019

66 Marijuana will be made available free on the NHS for the treatment of chronic diseases such as itchy scrot. **99**

Charles Dance as David Carlton in
Ali G Indahouse, 2002

66

Man, I remember when a dime
bag cost a dime.

99

Half Baked, 1998

"

Jay: [singing] Noinch, noinch, noinch, schmokin weed, schmokin' weed.

"

Clerks, 1994

66

Stephen Colbert: Have you ever
   acted [while] high?
Josh Rogen: For the last 20 years,
   exclusively.

99

Self-proclaimed weed lover Seth Rogen is interviwed
on *The Late Show with Stephen Colbert*, April 2019

"

The slowest-growing religion in the world – Dudeism. An ancient philosophy that preaches non-preachiness, practises as little as possible, and above all, uh... lost my train of thought there. Anyway, if you'd like to find peace on earth and goodwill, man, we'll help you get started. Right after a little nap.

"

Tenets of Dudeism, based on the life of the fictional pot smoker played by Jeff Bridges in the 1998 film *The Big Lebowski*

66

There is no attempt here to distance Wilson from the sex'n'drugs'n'rock'n'roll around him. He's shown as a connoisseur of the weed (though a particularly fine blend he thinks must be Caribbean is, in fact, from Rhyl).

99

Philip French discusses *24 Hour Party People* lead character Tony Wilson in *The Guardian*, 2002

"

We're just real Topeka people, man. Smoke some righteous weed.

"

Almost Famous, 2000

66

Sam Mendes reveals he got Kevin Spacey STONED for a key scene in *American Beauty*

99

Headline as seen on dailymail.co.uk
by Gaby Bissett, 31 May 2016

"

You get really stoned... Then, you know, like, who cares about the war? Heh... this war...

"

Unnamed American GI, 13 November 1970,
as quoted in "Shotgunning' weed in Vietnam",
Mashable, 20 April 2016. The scene was recreated in
the 1986 Oliver Stone film *Platoon*.

" The joint I'm about to roll requires a craftsman. It can utilize up to 12 skins. It is called a Camberwell Carrot... I invented it in Camberwell, and it looks like a carrot. "

Danny, *Withnail and I*, 1987

"

A 75-year-old ex-truck driver and his fortune-teller wife, 48, told police they were inspired by the British comedy film, *Saving Grace*, after they were caught growing cannabis in a rented warehouse.

"

"Italian Cannabis Growers 'Inspired' by British film",
The Local, 4 January 2015

"

Doug Benson's *Super High Me* knows exactly what its audience will be. This is a movie for people who f*@king love weed.

"

Christopher Monfette's review of *Super High Me*, as seen on ign.com, 13 May 2012

"

She was living in a single room
with three other individuals,
one of them was a male, and
the other two, well, the other
two were females. God only
knows what they were up to in
there, and furthermore, Susan, I
wouldn't be the least bit surprised
to learn that all four of them
habitually smoked marijuana
cigarettes... reefers.

"

Duncan McLeod as Porter Hall in
Beyond the Valley of the Dolls, 1970

"

We gotta stay loose. Let it cool, let the coolness get into our vertebrae.

"

Roman soldiers in *History of the World, Part 1*, 1981, who had been chasing down Mel Brooks and Gregory Hines in a high-speed chariot pursuit – when Hines spots a field of "Red Roman wacky weed", he uses papyrus to roll a giant joint and the billowing smoke turns the pursuing Romans pretty mellow...

CHAPTER
THREE

MUSIC

If humans have been smoking dope for 4,000 years, then the music created throughout that period will have been influenced by its purple haze...

The early stages of recorded
music saw classic pressings
from jazz's great musicians that
are littered with drug references.

Many of those listening to
the recordings would have been
unaware of what they were
hearing – and this is probably
still the case with people
listening today.

The jazz artists influenced by Caribbean culture, either directly or indirectly, went on to inspire the legends of Blues – who would in turn become the inspiration for rock and roll all the way through to today's chart-toppers.

Never mind the legions of artists who never strayed away from music's mainstream and lived among its underground roots.

While of course there will always be music free from weed's allure, no list of the greatest songs ever recorded, or the artists who made them, would be complete without some of the best "drug" songs of all time.

"

'Got to Get You into My Life' was one I wrote when I had first been introduced to pot.

"

Paul McCartney, *Many Years from Now*, 1997

66

I never have and never will write
a drug song.

99

Bob Dylan at London's Royal Albert Hall in May 1966,
though this hasn't stopped "Rainy Day Women
#12 and 35" becoming part of pot lore with its chorus
line "Everyone must get stoned"

"

The more you accept herb is the more you accept Rastafari.

"

Bob Marley

"

Herb is the healing of the nation, alcohol is the destruction.

"

Bob Marley

"

I mean herbs are good for everything. Why, why these people who want to do so much good for everyone, who call themselves governments and this and that. Why them say you must not use the herb? Them just say, 'No, you mustn't use it, you mustn't use it because it will make you rebel.' Against what?

"

Bob Marley in a New Zealand interview, 1979

"

The Beatles did it, Morrison did it and Black Sabbath went as far to write a love song for it. 'Sweet Leaf' is one of those classics whose lyrical content overshadows the actual music. There had been songs about drug effects earlier but never before was such a thing written...

...A song describing a person's infatuation with the sweet leaf, marijuana, was really something new.

"

Black Sabbath's "Sweet Leaf", 1971, as described by The Metal Archives in 2009

66

Tonight's the Night reaffirms Young's belief in the redemptive power of rock 'n' roll, but also in the consolation of marijuana.

99

Pot Culture reflects on the impact of Neil Young's album featuring the song "Roll Another Number (for the Road)", 1975

"

'Smoke Two Joints' gets bonus points for popping up in Kevin Smith's Gen-X classic *Mallrats*.

"

Sublime's 1992 cover of The Toyes' "Smoke Two Joints" features drug-related samples and bong rips throughout. It's a stoner classic.

66

Attention, hippies! There's an official Jimi Hendrix-brand cannabis vaporizer.

99

Rob Waugh, *Metro*, 2015, on the launch of purple Haze Sticks, which shows how weed's mythology can come from anywhere

"Purple Haze" the song has nothing to do with marijuana (disappointing, I know). It's to do with LCD. No, that's not true either. Apparently, it's a sci-fi reference. Hendrix originally wrote a much longer version of the song, with lyrics inspired by Philip José Farmer's novel *Night of Light: Day of Dreams*, that involve a "purplish haze" disorienting and transforming aliens on a distant planet. Many close to Jimi said he hadn't even tried acid at that point.

"

It's a trip that there's a category now called 'cannabis entertainment'. Before it was just about music. If you happened to mention cannabis within your music, it was still just music.

"

B-Real of Cypress Hill, whose songs include 1993's "Hits from the Bong", speaks to benzinga.com ahead of the latest weed-cooking show, *Bong Appétit*

"

You smoke bud and you turn into this philosopher.

"

Afroman, credited as being the first rapper to go
"viral before viral" on the two minutes it took him to
write the 2000 hit "Because I Got High"

"

I gave drugs a break for a while.
Except for acid, and mushrooms,
and lots and lots of weed.
That still counts as 'straight
edge', right?

"

Eric Melvin, guitar player of legendary punk
rockers NOFX, in *NOFX: The Hepatitis Bathtub and
Other Stories* by NOFX with Jeff Alulis, 2016

66

It really puzzles me to see marijuana connected with narcotics... dope and all that crap. It's a thousand times better than whiskey – it's an assistant – a friend.

99

Attributed to Louis Armstrong in reference to the drug culture in 1920s and '30s jazz

CHAPTER
FOUR

COMEDY

A drug that makes the monotonous and mundane seem like life-altering experiences, and the day-to-day fascinatingly other-worldly.

A chemically induced state that brings out the ridiculousness of everyday scenarios: it's as if cannabis was created by the almighty him/herself with comedy in mind. Heck, one of its more common side-(intended?) effects is to leave the user in a fit of giggles.

The comedian's audience is ALREADY LAUGHING. That said, the short-term memory loss that also goes with a high can make following a stand-up routine that little bit trickier.

"

And is there any negative effects?

"

Ali G, *Da Ali G Show*, 2003, after being told by a
Drug Enforcement Administration agent that cannabis
slows the brain and impairs learning

66

I don't do drugs though,
just weed.

99

Dave Chappelle as Thurgood Jenkins
in *Half Baked*, 1998

"

Grass, the word was out. Marijuana, MARIJUANA. Bush, hemp, boo smoke, weed, gage, grass, weed, Mary Jane??

'It's in all the books, Mary Jane, marijuana, nobody ever said it?'

"

George Carlin in *Toledo Window Box*, 1974

66

Marijuana will be legal someday, because the many law students who now smoke pot will one day be congressmen and they will legalize it to protect themselves.

99

Lenny Bruce, *How to Talk Dirty and Influence People*, 1965

66

The vape pen has changed my life. No, I'm not exaggerating. In fact, her name is Sippy. Yes, she's a she. And yes, I named her Sippy because I take tiny, little sips – sassy sips, even – from her. And with each sip comes relief – from pressure, pain, stress, discomfort.

99

Whoopi Goldberg in her debut blog
for The Cannabist, 17 April 2014

"

Aside from weed, which he very much enjoys and whose legalization he supports, and whiskey, which he enjoys maybe even more, and that awful brown toothpaste, Joe Rogan's body is a temple.

"

Devin Gordon on Joe Rogan in *The Atlantic*,
19 August 2019

66

I just ate pot and am gonna work out while watching @thegoodfight, will keep y'all posted.

99

Sarah Silverman, Twitter, 5 December 2018

"

I think the best part of this tweet is she forgot to keep us posted.

"

Jason Gaudion, referring to Sarah Silverman's tweet,
Twitter, 5 December 2018

66

I used to smoke marijuana. But I'll tell you something: I would only smoke it in the late evening. Oh, occasionally the early evening, but usually the late evening – or the mid-evening...

...Just the early evening, mid-evening and late evening. Occasionally, early afternoon, early mid-afternoon, or perhaps the late-mid-afternoon. Oh, sometimes the early-mid-late-early morning... But never at dusk.

99

Steve Martin

66

Democrats must get a good wedge issue to make sure they win the next election and I have one in mind. Hint: today is 4/20. The holiday where stoners everywhere smoke weed to celebrate smoking weed every other day of their lives.

99

Real Time with Bill Maher, HBO, 20 April 2018

66

Chelsea Handler wants to help get
your mom back into weed.

99

Zach Harris after the comedian launched
her own brand of cannabis products, as seen on
MerryJane.com, 31 May 2019

66

When you get stoned your discretion goes out the window. You can be eating kitty litter and you'll be going 'mmmm this is crunchy, man.'

99

Robin Williams, *A Night at the Met*, 1986

"

I love marijuana cuz it's giggly.

"

Joan Rivers, *Access Hollywood*, 2013

"

They lie about marijuana. Tell you pot-smoking makes you unmotivated. Lie! When you're high, you can do everything you normally do just as well — you just realize that it's not worth the fucking effort. There is a difference.

"

Bill Hicks, *Laughter and the Truth*, 2002

❝

Margaret [Cho] smoked out of the gorgeous peony-flowered bong I'd brought, and then draped herself across the bed in her luxury suite at the Borgata as we showered her with bud for the photo shoot.

❞

Interview with cannabis writer Mary Jane Gibson (yes, that's her real name), *Forbes*, 12 November 2019

"

In quite possibly the weirdest video interview concept ever, Jack Black got high on marijuana.

"

Tina Campbell, *Metro*, 29 September 2014

"

It has this grungy image, but it is as far away from being hedonistic and cool when you've watched your mum rub it on her feet.

"

"Russell Howard on his Mum, Cannabis and Getting Political", headline as seen on BT.com by Alex Fletcher, 26 March 2018

66

Comedian Billy Connolly tried cannabis to treat his Parkinson's disease — but reveals he ended up just getting stoned.

99

Rod McPhee, *The Sun*, 20 December 2018

CHAPTER
FIVE

CULTURE

Among purveyors
of pot's impact on
popular culture, few
days stand out in
the calendar quite
as much as 20 April.
How and why are
almost as transient
and hazy as the puffs
of smoke that fill the
air to mark the day.

So, at what point did the 20th day
of the 4th month of each year
become etched in resin?

There are more theories to this
as there are varietals of cannabis.
Some think it's a reference
to the code used by police
to indicate that somebody is
wacking the weed.

It isn't.

The more arithmetically minded have noted that it's a homage to the Bob Dylan classic "Rainy Day Women #12 & 35", because 12 x 35 = 420.

Except Bob says he's never written a song about marijuana and that the song title is a biblical reference.

According to *Time* magazine (the real one, not the pretend ones with fake Donald Trump covers), there is a much more likely source to the "stoner holiday".

An April 2018 article by reporter Olivia Waxman puts the source of the festival squarely on the shoulders of five students from St Rafael High School in California.

The students – Steve Capper, Dave Reddix, Jeffrey Noel, Larry Schwartz and Mark Gravich – would meet at the campus' statue of chemist Louis Pastuer at 4.20pm each day to smoke weed.

But why 4.20pm, you ask?

The timing was set for no other reason than that was when the school's activities ended and so it was the earliest they could meet for their own extracurricular activities.

4.

20

According to Dave Reddix, it was because they got bored of the jock-dominated Friday night football scene.

He told *Time* in 2017: "We were the guys sitting under the stands smoking a doobie, wondering what we were doing there."

But that doesn't explain how "420" then transcended the globe and permeated into weed culture.

So, the story continues…

Reddix's brother helped him land a job as a roadie for hippie favourites The Grateful Dead. With their fondness for the flower, the constantly touring band popularized the term among their legion of fans, dubbed Deadheads.

On 28 December 1990, the article concludes, a group of Deadheads were handing out flyers inviting people to smoke 420 on 20 April at 4.20pm.

One of these ended up in the hands of *High Times* reporter Steven Bloom, and the following year the magazine printed it and has been referencing the number ever since.

"

Marijuana is not a drug, it's
a leaf.

"

Arnold Schwarzenegger, *The Independent*,
29 October 2007

"

Not only can cannabis work for a variety of conditions such as epilepsy, multiple sclerosis and pain, sometimes, it is the only thing that works. I changed my mind, and I am certain you can, as well. It is time for safe and regulated medical marijuana to be made available nationally.

"

Leonard Barrett, *The Rastafarians; The Dreadlocks of Jamaica*, 1977

In 2019, Parkinson's UK carried out a study of 1,600 people with the condition and a further 29 healthcare professionals with the aim of learning their views and experience of using cannabis-derived products.

Parkinson UK's key findings were:

59% hadn't used cannabis before
but would consider it

26% had used cannabis,
16% currently do

16% hadn't and had no interest

According to the charity, people with Parkinson's would "overwhelmingly" continue to use, or start using, cannabis if evidence emerged that is was a safe and effective treatment.

"

When logic and proportion have
    fallen sloppy dead
And the white knight is talking
    backwards
And the red queen's off with her
    head
Remember what the dormouse
    said
Feed your head, feed your head

"

Lyrics from "White Rabbit" written by Grace Slick and recorded by Jefferson Airplane. The band was the first of the San Francisco psychedelic rock groups of the 1960s to achieve national recognition.

"

Rastafarians first began using
marijuana in reaction to the
treatment of blacks in society.
It became a reactionary device
to enable freedom from the
establishment.

"

Leonard Barrett, *The Rastafarians:*
The Dreadlocks of Jamaica, 1977

66

There is no evidence that
cannabis use actually causes...
later drug use.

99

Michelle Taylor, researcher at University of Bristol
studying cannabis, *The Guardian*, 3 March 2015

66

Mothers' milk, leads to everything.

99

George Carlin, *Toledo Window Box*, 1974

The cannabis experience has greatly improved my appreciation for art, a subject which I had never much appreciated before. The understanding of the intent of the artist which I can achieve when high…

...sometimes carries over to when I'm down. This is one of many human frontiers which cannabis has helped me traverse.

99

Carl Sagan on the virtues of marijuana, Keay Davidson, *Carl Sagan: A Life*, 1999

CHAPTER
SIX

POLITICS

To say politics has had a chequered history with marijuana would be to seriously undersell the story. Cannabis laws have tended to be based largely on the individual motivations of leaders rather than any substantive evidence – most strikingly in post-Prohibition USA.

Today, many a politician looks anything but comfortable when asked if they have ever tried cannabis or other drugs, often struggling to balance whether to appear human or "clean-living", which leads to some creative answers.

"

When I was a kid, I inhaled, frequently. That was the point.

"

Barack Obama, when running for president in 2008

❝ I wouldn't answer the marijuana
questions. You know why?
Because I don't want some little
kid doing what I tried. **❞**

George W. Bush in conversations secretly recorded
by biographer Douglas Wead, as seen on nytimes.com,
by David D. Kirkpatrick, 20 February 2005

66

When I was in England, I experimented with marijuana a time or two, and I didn't like it. I didn't inhale and never tried it again.

99

President Clinton on the election trail, 1992

66

Would you put a pastrami in your mouth if you didn't want to eat it?

99

Jackie Mason on Bill Clinton's admittance he tried marijuana but never inhaled, *An Equal Opportunity Offender*, 1995

"

The president smoked three of the six joints Mary brought to him. At first he felt no effects. Then he closed his eyes and refused a fourth joint. 'Suppose the Russians did something now,' he said.

"

Michael O'Brien, *John F. Kennedy: A Biography*, 2005

"

Marijuana smoking was 'about the only good thing' about the Mexican-American War.

"

Franklin Pierce, 14th president of the United States of America in a letter to his family

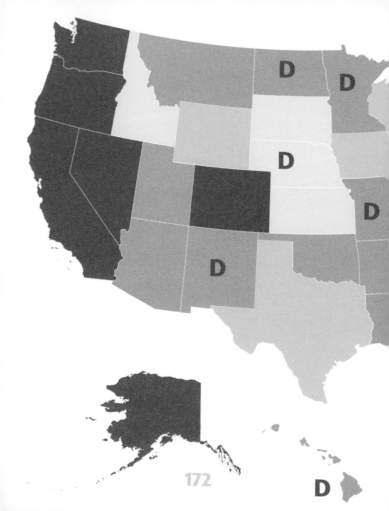

US States where it's legal to smoke weed

- ● Legal
- ● Legal for medicinal use
- ● Legal for medicinal use, limited THC content
- ● Prohibited for any use
- **D** Decriminalized

Source: National Conference of State Legislatures
1 August 2019

"

At university, I tried cannabis, not very often as I was into sport. It was a mistake, particularly the more I know now about the link between it and mental health issues.

"

Former UK Foreign Secretary Dominic Raab, as reported by *Sky News*, 2019

66

Cannabis – also called: Weed, Skunk, Sinsemilla, Sensi, Resin, Puff, Pot, Marijuana, Herb, Hashish, Hash, Grass, Ganja, Draw, Dope, Bud, Bhang, Pollen.

99

UK government website talktofrank.com, 2020

In 2014, police in County Durham, England, decided small-scale cannabis producers were no longer a priority, meaning those who grew for their own consumption would not be targeted.

That same year, Feed the Birds, a group promoting awareness of the benefits of the hemp seed, planted the herb next to iconic London landmarks such as Big Ben, Tower Bridge and the Shard in protest of cultivation laws.

Under current UK law, cannabis is different to other Class B drugs as it comes under the discretionary warning scheme.

This means that a police officer can choose to issue you with a street warning only (which doesn't form a criminal record, though it will be recorded), so long as: you're in possession of a small amount of cannabis only and for your personal use; it's the first time you've been caught with an illicit drug and you have no previous record of offence; and you are compliant, non-aggressive and admit that the cannabis is for your own use only.

If you're caught with cannabis and it's your second offence, the police can issue you with a fixed-term fee notice, an on-the-spot fine for £80.

As long as the fine is paid within 21 days, there's no criminal record.

If there's a third occasion, you will be arrested.

"

There is clear scientific and medical evidence that cannabis is a harmful drug which can damage people's mental and physical health, and harms individuals and communities. We have no plans to change the law.

"

Conservative party spokesperson,
as seen on *bbc.co.uk* by Tomas Frymorgen, 6 June 2017

66

We do not support the legalization of cannabis. Our goal is to see fewer people start using drugs, more people helped by treatment towards a drug-free life, and a reduction in the damage which problem drug users can cause to communities.

99

Labour party spokesperson,
as seen on *bbc.co.uk* by Tomas Frymorgen, 6 June 2017

66

The SNP are not in favour of
general decriminalization of
cannabis, but clearly there is a
specific case for medicinal use –
such as in the case of Sativex,
a cannabis-based medicine
used to treat MS and available
on the NHS.

99

Scottish National Party spokesperson,
as seen on *bbc.co.uk* by Tomas Frymorgen, 6 June 2017

I can confirm that we support the legalization of cannabis for medicinal use, and that we have worked with the police and prime pommissioners on this issue.

Plaid Cymru, as seen on *bbc.co.uk* by
Tomas Frymorgen, 6 June 2017

"

Let's legalise cannabis... Back the Liberal Democrats' plan to break the grip of criminal gangs and protect young people by introducing a legal, regulated market for cannabis.

"

Petition on the Liberal Democrats Website, 2020

66

Cannabis would be removed from the 1971 Misuse of Drugs Act. The possession, trade and cultivation of cannabis would be immediately decriminalized, roughly following the Dutch model. The trade in cannabis would be the subject of a Royal Commission... with a view to establishing a fully legalized, controlled and regulated trade.

99

Green party policy statement,
as seen on *bbc.co.uk* by Tomas Frymorgen, 6 June 2017

And what about Amsterdam?

Its drug laws are at best hazy...

It is not legal to smoke marijuana
in the Netherlands.

This despite the proliferation of
coffeeshops that sell cannabis
over the counter.

Weed, however, is tolerated
with a "blind eye" turned towards
those carrying fewer than
5 grams (0.1 ounces).

The coffeeshops themselves
are licensed to trade by
the authorities and can store
up to 500 grams (17½ ounces)
of cannabis on the premises at
any one time.

The popularity of the shops has
become so great among tourists
that the Dutch government is now
considering restricting them to
the locals only.

66

Marijuana never kicks down your door in the middle of the night. Marijuana... does not suppress medical research, does not peek in bedroom windows. Even if one takes every reefer madness allegation of the prohibitionists at face value, marijuana prohibition has done far more harm to far more people than marijuana ever could.

99

Conservative commentator William Buckley, Jr

"

40 million Americans smoked marijuana; the only ones who didn't like it were Judge Ginsberg, Clarence Thomas and Bill Clinton.

"

Jay Leno

192